Breakthrough to Entrepreneurial Brilliance

Shatter the Invisible Barrier Holding Your Business Back

Alana Mills

Difference Press

Washington, DC, USA

Copyright © Alana Mills, 2024

All rights reserved. No part of this book may be reproduced in any form without permission in writing from the author. Reviewers may quote brief passages in reviews.

ISBN: 978-1-68309-305-3

Published 2024

DISCLAIMER

No part of this publication may be reproduced or transmitted in any form or by any means, mechanical or electronic, including photocopying or recording, or by any information storage and retrieval system, or transmitted by email without permission in writing from the author.

Neither the author nor the publisher assumes any responsibility for errors, omissions, or contrary interpretations of the subject matter herein. Any perceived slight of any individual or organization is purely unintentional. Brand and product names are trademarks or registered trademarks of their respective owners.

DELIBERATE CREATOR PROCESS BY ALANA M™ is a registered trademark of Alana Mills.

Cover design: Jennifer Stimson

Editing: Madeline Kosten

Author photo courtesy of: Brisbane Headshots

This book is dedicated to every woman who is destined to create an impact – leaders, visionaries, entrepreneurs, and innovators!
You are the change makers who make this world a better place!

Contents

Author's Note	vii
Introduction: Is This Book for You?	xi
1. My Story	1
2. Seasons of Change and Discovery	11
3. The Truth about How Life Really Works	23
4. You Can't Think Your Way Out of a Feeling Problem	37
5. How You Went from Fearless to Fearful – The Power of the Subconscious Mind	49
6. The False Self vs. the True Self	65
7. What You Need to Give up to Be a "Deliberate Creator"	75
8. The Secret to True Power and Freedom	83
9. For Such a Time as This (From the Ancient Hebrew Book of Esther)	91
Afterword	97
Acknowledgments	101
About the Author	103
About Difference Press	105
Other Books by Difference Press	109
Thank You!	111

Author's Note

You are reading these words knowing from your earliest memories you were destined to be a powerful female leader. It's part of your soul; it's in your DNA. Being a leader feels as natural as breathing. You know what it feels like to lead, to have wins in business, and to be successful, yet there is something missing, something you just can't put your finger on. You are successful, yet you feel unfulfilled in your current business or life situation.

You know you are destined for more!

This is the book I wish someone would have given to me thirty-two years ago when I birthed my first business. I have included some of my own life story within these pages in the hopes that you will be able to resonate with it. Contained inside this book are the challenges I faced in my endless search for true fulfillment and freedom and ultimately my journey in awakening to my true leadership power and potential!

As you read through these pages, I reveal the secrets to the truth about how life really works and the truth of how powerful we women really are as leaders. I will discuss what it really means to design your destiny and create the business and life you really want.

It is achieved through my very own trademarked DELIBERATE CREATOR PROCESS BY ALANA M™ that I developed from working with women who struggled, knowing they were leaders and entrepreneurs, but wanting more in life with the goal of mental clarity and emotional and financial freedom.

The common desire that the women I work with crave is *freedom*. Freedom from the self-sabotaging thought patterns that run daily in their minds, freedom to trust their intuition in decision-making, freedom to process the emotions that keep them stopped, stuck, and struggling. and financial freedom to live the life they have always wanted.

Freedom to be the creators of their destiny, achieved through my trademarked methodology.

DELIBERATE CREATOR PROCESS BY ALANA M™ is the exact process that transformed me from the shy, fearful and self-doubting Alana, constantly feeling like I was at the mercy of everyone and everything and that "life was just happening to me" to the confident, leader I am today. I awakened to the truth of how powerful it feels to be deliberately creating and living my destiny, leaving the impact I am here to make, empowering women like you to do the same.

Introduction: Is This Book for You?

I grew up in the 1970s on a rural Australian cattle property and was home-schooled until age ten. As such when I started to attend mainstream school, I was a shy, quiet girl, who always wanted to speak up but never had the confidence to do it!

I was smart and loved studying, but I struggled to make friends in those first years. I always felt I had more to give and knew the answers in class but wouldn't put up my hand for fear of judgement from my peers! *If I got the answer wrong, what would they think?*

Even as a child, I knew that I wanted to be a change maker, to make a positive impact in the world, to be a leader. At seventeen, I left home to attend university and study business with the intention of founding a business of my own.

At the age of twenty-one, in the early 1990s, this dream became a reality and within a couple of years, I was the proud owner of a successful beauty therapy business. Clients would say to me, "You must feel super successful at your age having your own business."

I would simply acknowledge and reply, "Absolutely!"

But behind the scenes, I felt anything but successful *and* knew I wanted to go all in and take my business to the next level. I would get to a certain point and feel like I had hit an invisible wall, then I would make excuses in my mind to justify that it was easier to stay small. This inevitably left me feeling frustrated and unfulfilled.

Fast forward thirty-two years and life is very different now in the business world; it's way tougher than it was in the nineties. With so many brands vying for our attention, in order to be globally recognized, we have to deliver our brand with complete clarity, and it has to wow the customer/client so much so that they can't live another day without acquiring what we offer!

Introduction: Is This Book for You?

Or in the words from the 1989 movie, *When Harry Met Sally*, "I'll have what she is having!"

You are reading this because you know you are a leader, and a change maker! You are passionate about living your full potential and making an impact in the world. You may already be doing something that you love, or you might have this amazing idea about creating a business with your own unique brand, using your unique 'zone of genius' to create the business you have always dreamed of. Yet, you feel like something is stopping you from really "going all in" to create the business and life you have always wanted.

You get to a certain point and then feel stuck, stopped, and struggling like you have hit an invisible wall you just can't break though.

Maybe you can relate to what I experienced as CEO of my business so many years ago.

I wanted to expand my business and charge more for my expertise, but the fear of judgement and failure kept me stuck.

I wanted to be a more confident leader and communicator, but certain people (personality types) scared the hell out of me, and I felt powerless in their energy.

I was constantly comparing myself and my

brand and never felt like I could never be as amazing or successful as others were.

I felt caught in a cycle of wanting more, only to go one step forward and two steps back, as if I was self-sabotaging my success.

What the hell was wrong with me!?

I had been to university and studied business. I knew I wasn't unintelligent. I was driven! I knew I had strong leadership qualities and was skilled at what I did but still felt like I would get to a certain level in my business only to hit a wall.

What did the top 2 to 5 percent of the population who were millionaires and multi-millionaires know that I didn't? Worse still, *how much would I have to invest to ever find out?* I always felt the *real* reason I feared stepping into my true potential and going all in was yet to be revealed to me – whatever the heck that was!

This cycle continued until I finally discovered the reason for my invisible barrier and it wasn't what I thought it was!

It wasn't logical; it was emotional!

You are reading this today because you are a leader, knowing you are destined for more in business and in life. My mission is to awaken women to be the deliberate creators of their destiny, stepping

Introduction: Is This Book for You?

into their true leadership potential and uncovering the real reason they are not getting the results they desire in business and life.

Now at fifty-three, I am living an amazing life. I am a motivational speaker and life transformation expert. My bigger purpose is to empower female leaders like you to become a deliberate creator of your destiny, designing the business and life of your dreams through my proven, trademarked methodology DELIBERATE CREATOR PROCESS BY ALANA M™. This methodology has been designed to awaken you to your true power and live your full potential, and consider that a methodology is simply a recipe, and the steps are the ingredients required to achieve an amazing outcome! To fulfill your deepest desire in finding true emotional fulfillment and financial freedom, and to deliver your brand to the world with clarity, power, and confidence, making the impact you are here to make

Throughout the pages of this book, I will discuss the subconscious secrets to being the deliberate creator you are destined to be the coach, the leader, the entrepreneur operating within your "zone of genius," to make the impact you are here to make.

Introduction: Is This Book for You?

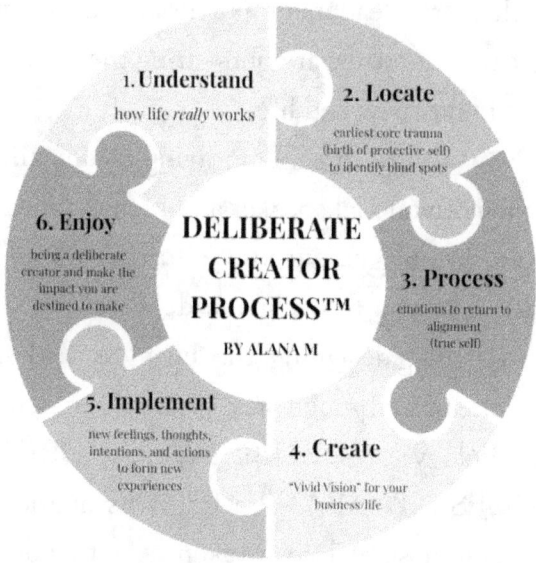

Together, I will walk you through the DELIBERATE CREATOR PROCESS BY ALANA M™, and you will:

1. Understand how life really works.
2. Locate your earliest core trauma (birth of protective self) to identify your blind spots.
3. Process your emotions to return to alignment (your true self).
4. Create your "vivid vision" for your business and life.

Introduction: Is This Book for You?

5. Implement your new feelings, thoughts, intentions, and actions to form new experiences.
6. Enjoy being a deliberate creator and make the impact you are destined to make.

The women I coach have always known their deepest desire was to live their full potential in business and life and be confident, powerful leaders, but felt there was a missing piece to the puzzle for them to feel truly fulfilled. They know they are here to create a positive impact and are not content with the status-quo.

They have read books on business and leadership, maybe even been to university, done self-improvement courses, and tried to change their mindsets, only to still feel like they missed the mark.

As I did, they went one step forward and two steps back, stuck in a loop of frustration, disempowerment, and overwhelm feeling unable to lead with true power and confidence to get the results they desire.

Breakthrough to Entrepreneurial Brilliance is for you if you aren't living your full potential and

Introduction: Is This Book for You?

achieving the results you desire in business and life because fear and self-doubt are holding you back.

This book will help you uncover the *real* reason – it's not what you think it is – you are trapped in this self-perpetuating cycle of taking one step forward and two steps back.

I will help awaken you to how you can free yourself from that trap, find mental clarity, emotional fulfillment and financial freedom to be the deliberate creator of your destiny.

To step into your true power and become the confident powerful leader you are born to be through my trademarked methodology, finally getting the results you have always wanted in business and life.

This is the book I wish someone had given me to read thirty-two years ago!

Chapter 1

My Story

"We are all storytellers, there isn't a stronger connection between people than telling their story."

— Jimmy Neil Smith

Life on the Land

Before I discuss the real reason we have this invisible barrier that keeps us stopped, stuck, and struggling, unable to truly harness our innate power to reach our true leadership potential and get the results we want in business and life, I need to share my story in more depth.

From my earliest memories growing up on a rural cattle property in Queensland, Australia, I remember being shy. Where we lived was over thirty minutes drive from the nearest neighbouring property. I distinctly remember the day we got electricity connected to our house. Prior to that, we ran our lights from a generator and cooked over a wood stove. Nowadays we would have described it as "living off grid."

Electricity meant a whole new world for us all that solved all sorts of obstacles the generator posed. I loved books and would often read before bed; however, this was fraught with complications when we had the generator as the only power source. As it was only run during the day, it meant bit-by-bit, the brightness emitted from my bedroom's only light bulb would slowly ebb away until there was no light left. No matter, I always had a torch (as long as the batteries were working).

With only my mum, dad, and my older brother to oversee the running of the property, there was always something to do. So much so that as kids, we would never say we were bored in front of my dad, as we would quickly be assigned a chore to do. One favourite chore of his to assign was to get us to clean out the back of the cattle truck, which involved shoveling and scraping cattle and horse manure off the wooden floor and side walls. Not my favourite chore and to this day, when I am driving on an outback highway and pass a cattle truck, the memories and the smell come flooding back.

Because the property sprawled over 100,000 acres of land, this meant all the roads around were unsealed, dirt roads with waterways (creeks) to cross, often without bridges. This meant when the wet season hit, days and even weeks would go by before we had any face-to-face contact with anyone outside of my family. Life was busy and like all land holders, we experienced good and bad seasons. I remember the drought times in particular trying to keep the horses and cattle alive with limited feed and water. It was all-hands-on-deck which meant days were spent feeding hay and molasses (which helps replace missing sugars and trace minerals in animals' diets) up to a 1,000 head of cattle just to keep them alive.

When the dams would get low in their water levels and the animals were weak from the drought, sometimes we would find them too late. They would get stuck in the mud trying to access less muddy water from the dam's edge and be too weak to get themselves out. As a young girl, I would always find this quite distressing, and I recall one such occasion when my brother and I came across a cow who had passed away in the muddy dam. Because he was older, my brother drove the vehicle and my job was to wade into the mud to secure the dead animal to a tow rope in order to remove her body from the mud. I am guessing I was around seven or eight years old. That was a part of life on a rural Australian cattle property.

In saying that I loved the animals, my main socializing was with the horses and cows. I remember having my first horse at age three. His name was Tiny and you might have guessed he was a Shetland pony (albeit a very moody pony at times). The simplicity of this was wonderful as they didn't care if I showed up like and acted the fool in front of them. If they were getting fed or brushed, I had a captive audience who loved me!

Being homeschooled via what was called "correspondence school" meant little interaction with the outside world and I remember the day we enrolled in the program called "School of the Air."

The School of the Air program involved having one half-hour lesson daily via a CB radio with a teacher and class of students from all over Queensland. Today we would call it a Zoom lesson call with audio only. The questions revolved around the papers we were working on and generally included math, English, and what we called social studies (history, geography, and economics). Each week we had a workbook or paper that had to be filled out and sent into the school's head office. It would be marked (I still remember the red pen lines and comments) and sent back to us. I know, this is unthinkable now with the technology we have.

I was scared stiff of these lessons as it was quite similar to a regular classroom with up to thirty children of similar ages and grades combined in a half-hour lesson. The format went something like this: a question was asked, and we had to press the button on the radio receiver and call out our name if we knew the answer.

I froze!

Even if I did know the answer, my anxiety would override this urge before I could even press the button.

Someone else always got to say the correct answer instead and I wanted so much to be confident and put myself out there like most of the other kids, but I just didn't know how.

I would spend ages psyching myself up before the lesson so I might be able to summon up the courage to press the button and try to formulate some intelligible answer in front of my peers, but it rarely happened.

I was always glad when the lesson was over and loved the morning time slots, so the lesson was done for the day, and so would be my anxiety, at least until the next day!

With the advent of my brother beginning high school (grade eight and upwards) and the ongoing demands of operating the family property to provide a profitable income stream for our family, it was not viable for my mum to keep home-schooling us both. She was very hands-on in the daily operation and like all of us, she helped outdoors and with the household duties such as cooking, etc.

The only option was for my brother and I to attend mainstream school. Fortunately, there was a school bus that had begun operating a twenty-minute drive from our property, so it was decided. *Mainstream school, here we come.* And yes, often my brother and I had the added responsibility of driving ourselves to the bus and leaving the vehicle in a neighbour's tractor shed until the journey home. After all, we had learnt to drive by age twelve or so, so in essence this was not a big deal for us. Again, unthinkable today, I know.

I was about to be flung into a world that was totally foreign to me, a real school with real teachers and students, not just my mum and a voice over a radio.

School Days

I was shy, but clever, and had a thirst for knowledge of any kind. My mum had been a great teacher and always ensured we got our lessons done – not just done, but done well. So much so that when I attended mainstream school, I was put up two grades (levels) for English and math class and would often be in a classroom with children at least two years older than me. This was daunting enough in itself and seemed to naturally exacerbate by fear of judgement and self-doubt.

When the teachers would ask for hands up to answer questions, I would quickly think, *I know this*, but would continue to run the same pattern I had always run.

I was so shy that I remember one day coming back into the classroom from play break. I hadn't realized I should have gone to the toilet and this mistake meant I sat in what started as discomfort and ended in agony, as I tried to keep my bladder from leaking onto the chair!

Too late, and to my embarrassment, I couldn't hold my full bladder anymore, much to my embarrassment, still to this day!

All because of my fear of speaking up and being judged for not having gone to the bathroom in my break.

As I entered into my final year of primary school, the position of school captain came up and I was nominated, not because of my leadership skills but I think it was because I always tried my best and was kind to the other students and yes, you guessed it, I actually got the position. *What the...!* Thank God it mainly involved looking out for the younger kids in the lower grades and helping around the school. However, this was my first break at a leadership position! In hindsight, I don't remember stuffing it up too much. I guess I was the quiet achiever or maybe no one else in the class wanted to do it.

Or maybe I was born to lead after all!

Eleven Years Later

As mentioned at the beginning of this book, I started my own business at twenty-one, bringing my leadership passion to the fore like never before. I loved it – the freedom and excitement of owning my own business. Over the years as my business grew, I expanded my brand, hired more staff, and life was good. I knew I was crushing it and then I would hit an invisible wall, feeling like I just couldn't go any further. *What the hell was wrong with me?* I wanted to have the courage to step into my power and take my business to the next level, but I continued to run the pattern of my young schoolgirl self. *What if I fail? What will people think?* Or conversely, what if I am mega successful? What will people think? Crazy, isn't it? I decided it was simply easier to stay safe and stay small. After all, I was successful, wasn't I? Yes, but I still wasn't fulfilled.

Then almost overnight, life's circumstances changed for me so dramatically I was forced to uncover the real reason for the invisible barrier that kept me small, because as I will discuss in the next chapter, the rest of my life depended on it!

Chapter 2

Seasons of Change and Discovery

"You cannot change the circumstances, the seasons or the wind, but you can change yourself. That is something you have charge of."

— Jim Rohn

By this stage, I had sold my business as I felt called to work with women who were vulnerable, those who were financially disadvantaged and socially marginalized due to life circumstances. I worked within a globally recognized organization called The Salvation Army or "Salvos" for short, employed in a leadership position managing an op shop and community centre where people could access affordable clothing, furniture, and household items as well as access to short-term accommodation and refuge from domestic violence.

In addition, I was also responsible (in part) for meeting the emotional and spiritual needs of those who required it. Although the workload was extremely demanding, especially with the demands of being a mum as well, I enjoyed providing support and meeting the practical and emotional needs of women and giving them hope for the future. The needs of the communities that I served were always great and I often felt under-resourced, both financially and practically.

I recall one particular occasion when a young woman walked into the centre that I managed. She looked like someone had squeezed almost every inch of life out of her. I escorted her to a private office and asked her to sit down. I enquired as to how I could help.

She spoke without emotion, in an almost robotic fashion, "I was wondering if you could help me, my baby died a couple of days ago and I have no money to bury him."

My heart broke and tears still well up today as I write these words. That image will stay in my mind forever. I had little resources, but I did what I could that day to help her.

To try and balance my stress levels, I studied to become an internationally qualified fitness professional through the global fitness cartel, Les Mills (no relation). My side hustle instructing fitness classes was a nice distraction and release from the demands of my full-time work.

However, the ongoing stress started to affect not only my health but also my relationship and after nineteen years of marriage, I was facing a divorce.

Tough Times

By now, I was in my mid-forties, with three beautiful daughters, facing a change of address, a change of career, and a divorce.

Whoa, that's a lot!

And yes, you are correct, it was a lot.

I wasn't the first woman to face this and certainly won't be the last. The reason I am telling you this is because I endured a five-year legal battle with my ex-husband over a property settlement and custody arrangements with our girls. I was feeling burnt out, and had lost my sense of identity, my confidence, and my desire to ever be in the spotlight again.

It was at this time that my side hustle as an internationally qualified fitness coach became my primary income stream.

I remember one morning standing on an instructor's stage in front of approximately forty women, mic'd up, about to lead a fitness class when I thought I was literally going to die! It began with breaking out into a sweat, and as I looked across the room full of women, I somehow felt disconnected from reality, as if the room was going to swallow me up. I had an incredible urge to drop my barbell and run out of the room to the front exit door, never to return.

If you have ever had a panic attack you will know that is exactly what it feels like.

I managed to focus on my breathing, and this enabled me to keep it together to finish the class, but I was utterly exhausted and knew I couldn't continue like this. It was as if that invisible barrier had popped up again, forcing me to doubt myself, my leadership capabilities, and the decisions I made. Nothing had worked in the past to free me from this invisible trap that kept me stopped, stuck, and struggling, and now it seemed more real and paralysing than ever.

Little did I know, very soon there was worse to come four years later.

Get Up, Straighten Your Crown, and Become All You Were Destined to Be

So many times I had felt like giving up while fighting for my divorce settlement. I had been to counselling, which helped to a degree, but it felt like I was struggling more than ever from fear and self-doubt It was then that one night, towards the early hours of the morning, that I had an impactful dream.

In my dream, I clearly saw a vision of a broken, grief-stricken woman. She had long, thick hair tied up in a bun with streaks of mascara running down her tear-stained face. Where her hair was once neat and pulled tightly on top of her head, it was now messy and straggly. I looked and she had a beautiful crystal tiara atop her head, but it was so crooked I feared it would fall and shatter into tiny pieces.

She was sobbing and with every sob, the sight of her became more and more desperate and bedraggled. She seemed so alone and hopeless. In my dream, I called out to her repeatedly, trying to offer her help. Why couldn't she hear me? This seemed to go on for ages, as if there was an invisible barrier between us. In my dream I was thinking, perhaps I'm just watching a movie, but as I slept, I could feel the emotion of the woman so intensely. Her depth of hopelessness and grief was almost too much to bear. I just wanted the dream to end. It felt both exhausting and heartbreaking.

Just when I felt I couldn't take any more and somehow needed to find a way to escape from this vivid dream, a voice came loud and clear to pierce the sound of the sobbing. It wasn't my voice; it was from somewhere else, saying, "Get up, straighten your crown, and become all you were destined to be!" It was so clear and I wasn't sure where it was coming from, but was so powerful that it woke me up with a jolt. The words were still as clear as ever in my mind, "Get up, straighten your crown, and become all you were destined to be." As you have probably guessed, the woman in the dream was me, in my desperate state of confusion and grief. The crooked crystal tiara represented the woman that felt beaten down by life and had lost her self-worth, her true identity, like so many women, who know they are meant for so much more in life but feel lost and disempowered. This vision had been so powerful that it awakened me to the fact that I knew this was not who I was destined to be.

I had always known I was on this earth to create an impact, that there was more to this life, and without a doubt, there was more ahead for me. Even though every fibre of my being felt broken and beaten down, and I felt like giving up, this vision was the turning point in my life I had been so desperately seeking. It seemed so real that even as I write these words today it is still so clear and powerful so many years later.

From that moment on, I was determined to become the woman who I knew I had been created to be: a confident leader, a change maker in an ever-evolving world fraught with chaos and uncertainty. I searched for the truth to how life really works, how our "false or protective self" (ego) is formed from our earliest core trauma and how this trauma is the catalyst for the self-sabotaging belief patterns that play out in our daily lives as we mature into adults. This is why we often go one step forward and two steps back, hitting an invisible barrier that we can't seem to break through. It is not until this trauma is identified that we can fully process our emotions to return to our true self, and be truly free to be powerful, confident leaders we were destined to be.

To this day, I still visualize this picture, but not as it appeared in the dream, The woman (me) has awakened to her true worth and her true power and the metaphorical crystal tiara is no longer crooked, but sitting proudly atop her head as the woman who lives her true purpose.

This is where the magic begins and that is why I developed DELIBERATE CREATOR PROCESS BY ALANA M™, a simple yet profound methodology outlined below to return to your true power and finally get the results you have always wanted in your business and life. The best part is you can actually find real joy and fulfillment in the process of making your vision reality as you deliberately design and create the impact you are here to make, through the following six steps:

- Understand how life really works.
- Locate your earliest core trauma (birth of protective self) to identify your blind spots.
- Process your emotions to return to alignment and harmony (your true

self).
- Create your "vivid vision" for your business and life.
- Implement your new feelings, thoughts, intentions, and actions to form new experiences.
- Enjoy being a deliberate creator and make the impact you are destined to make.

Become a Deliberate Creator

After years of battling for my property settlement post-divorce to be heard in the federal and family law court system, the day finally arrived when all eyes would be on me!

This was the crucial day when I would be cross-examined by my ex-husband's barrister in front of a high-level judge, the man who had the power to decide my future. It was interesting to note that the original judge who was presiding over the case was changed three days before my hearing. I didn't let it phase me as I knew this was totally out of my control. We will discuss the perception or illusion of control in the coming chapters.

I knew I had only one chance to take the stand and I had to be poised, composed, and deliver my answers with absolute clarity and confidence!

I was called to the stand (witness box) and after roughly a half hour of questioning, which seemed like a lifetime, I walked back to my seat between my lawyer and barrister!

What had just happened to me?!

I had just answered every question with complete composure, incredible confidence, and perfect clarity. So much so that my ex-husband's barrister seemed caught off guard and cut the cross-examination short as she replied to the judge, "No more questions Your Honour."

It seemed like an eternity (for me anyway) as we awaited the judge's comments.

The outcome that followed seemed surreal!

The judge was in favour of my evidence, and the way I was able to answer every question so confidently and concisely.

I was silently confident and even more so when my barrister leaned in and said to me at the conclusion of the hearing, "If we don't win this, I'll eat my hat!"

A few weeks later, the judge's ruling was emailed to me via my lawyers, and the good news was that my barrister did not have to follow through on his promise.

We had won the case, and I was ecstatic, as this was not only a new beginning for me being finally free from my past, but also because I knew with certainty I had finally and successfully broken through my invisible barrier of fear and self-doubt! I finally felt free of the invisible trap that had held me captive for so long. I felt confident, capable, and powerful! I had won my case and it had paid off (in the form of a substantial six-figure payment) immensely for me, not only financially, but also mentally and emotionally.

In that one moment, I knew what it was really like to be a deliberate creator and to operate from a place of true power and self -worth and I had the results to prove it!

My life's mission became crystal clear. My bigger purpose is to coach women who know they are born leaders to awaken and live their full potential from their true power and self- worth to create the business and life they have always wanted thereby becoming the deliberate creators of their destiny using the six steps outlined in my trademarked methodology to finally get the results they have always desired in business and life.

Chapter 3

The Truth about How Life Really Works

"The greatest power a person possesses is the power to choose!"

— J Martin Kohe

I'm going to now share with you how life really works as we dive into Step 1 in becoming the deliberate creator of your destiny. This is integral to understanding how to "go all in" to get the results you want in life and business.

You might be thinking, *Alana, what do you mean by "how life really works"?*

I'm glad you asked!

I want you to consider something, "Does life work inside out or outside in?"

Let me illustrate – consider the device on which you are reading these words, whether a smartphone, or iPad, computer, or a printed page.

Wasn't it once an idea in the inventor's mind? IBM was the first designer of the smartphone. In 1993, it was sold by BellSouth and included a touchscreen interface for accessing its calculator, calendar, address book, and other functions.

The reason I am telling you this is because that idea had to be held as an intention, then from the intention, plans were developed, technology needed to be implemented, and so on until the first smartphone was successfully patented and marketed for sale.

With the illustration I have just provided, consider that life really works **from the inside out!**

For the majority of my life, I had got it wrong. I used to think that life worked *from the outside in* and felt that life was just happening to me, as if I was at the mercy of everyone and everything around me. Stuck in the trap of trying to attain my self-worth from others, by people pleasing, and saying yes to things I really wanted to say no to!

I felt alone and disconnected from who I really was, from other people, and from this crazy ride called life.

I was the worst control freak in the world, thinking I had to micromanage everyone and everything around me, and it was *exhausting*!

As such, I never trusted myself, always had self-doubt, and constantly beat up on myself for not going all in to get the results I truly desired in business and life. It seemed as if I was in this self-sabotaging cycle of gaining momentum just to hit a wall time and time again, only to "rinse and repeat" the never-ending cycle – when in fact, I had all the *power* to create my reality from the inside out but *none* of the control.

What?!

Think back to the illustration I gave you of the first smartphone and how it evolved into reality.

Everything in life, including the chair you are sitting on, the appliances in your home, and the clothes and shoes you are wearing were once an idea in someone's mind that was held as an intention.

That intention was followed through until it became reality, a tangible object.

Wait, Alana, are you saying we create our own reality?!

Absolutely, that is exactly what I am saying, whether we do it consciously or by default, either way, we can do nothing but create!

This is achieved through the power of choice.

Every day we have the power of choice; we choose to get up out of bed, or not.

We choose to do our morning walk, run, gym routine, or not.

We choose to go to work, or not.

I am not saying there aren't consequences for our choices, I am just saying, we do have the power of choice.

Conversely, we can't control anything!

When was the last time you controlled the weather?

When was the last time you controlled gravity?

When was the last time you controlled the stock market or interest rates?

It is an illusion that we can really control any situation in life.

And knowing we have all the *power* and none of the control is incredibly freeing!

Knowing that we can deliberately create our reality, though the power of choice (where our real power lies) day in and day out, this the gold we are searching for.

Stay with me as I am building a foundation on which you can really understand and uncover the real reason you hold fear and self-doubt in trusting yourself to "go all in" in business and life.

Essentially there are only two rules or laws which are the foundation of creating the results you desire which we will discuss now.

Universal Law of Cause and Effect

The first is the Universal Law of Cause and Effect.

The Universal Law of Cause and Effect states that nothing – absolutely nothing – is happening by chance.

For every effect, there is a definite cause, and similarly for every cause, there is a definite effect.

For every action, there is an equal and opposite reaction or consequence.

Maybe you have heard of this before?

This means that your thoughts, feelings, behaviours, and actions create definite effects that manifest and create your reality and in turn the results you get or don't get in life.

The foundational understanding in this is that it is an equal opportunity law!

This means it doesn't differentiate between what you say you want or say you don't want.

Another way of putting it is, whatever you think about, and from there internalize, will become the effects of this, because it is law. To illustrate this, according to best-selling author and speaker Esther (Abraham) Hicks, it takes just seventeen seconds of focusing on a thought before another of its kind comes to mind. So, if we constantly doubt our ability to complete a task or make a decision, another thought will add to that doubt and so on building momentum., Even as I write these words, I recall times, when I stuffed up big time (or so I thought) and in my perception I equated the "stuff ups" with my sense of worth and would mentally "beat myself up" by thinking thoughts of "not being good enough, or smart enough." You know it, we all do it, and consider how quickly those thoughts gain momentum and pretty soon, the thoughts become a belief we hold about ourselves, which does nothing but erode our self-trust.

When, in reality all negative experiences or so called 'stuff ups' are just feedback. When we can take the big picture view and look at the experience as an observer (more on that later), we are able to break down the experience into what worked, what didn't work, and what would could be changed to create a different experience in the same context. In other words, get curious and ask yourself, does this experience define me or is this just feedback so I can re adjust whatever I need and go again to create differently!

For so much of my life, I couldn't fully trust myself to make big business and life decisions, and when I did, I would be caught up in a viscous cycle of second-guessing and doubting what I had done. True to this law, it only created more second-guessing and doubt creating less and less trust in my capability to make confident decisions.

Conversely, if we think we are capable of completing a task or making a decision, and fully trust ourselves, another thought will add to quickly building our self-trust and confidence. Either way, we will always create more of what we internalize, as this is an equal opportunity law!

Have you ever played the game of tug of war? It was a game I used to play at school camps and involved a very thick, strong battle rope with a tape mark in the centre and two teams equally numbered on either side of the rope. The game is won when the strongest team pulls the other team successfully over a line that is marked on the ground. In order to win, the strategy was always to have the strongest kids on your team. I was always quite small and thin in high school and in hindsight may well have been the weakest link in the team. Needless to say, I don't remember winning often.

This game is always an interesting spectator sport as two well-opposed teams might spend quite some time fighting it out to the end. I liken this to how I would play the game of business and life. There were times when I felt like I was crushing it, only to feel a sense of overwhelm and defeat in hitting my invisible wall and being pulled back across the line.

Let me illustrate – we cannot get the results we want in business while we secretly internalize our fear of "going all in" or stepping into our true power (most times this shows up as fear of judgement and / or failure) as this would defy this Universal Law of Cause and Effect. This is not about morality, or right or wrong. This is just how this law works and more importantly, how life *really* works.

The more we hold fear of anything in life, the more that fear gains momentum.

And consider that you are reading the words on these pages because you know you are a born leader and change- maker. When you have the gift of leadership, you cannot help but lead, problem-solve and create positive change. Knowing you were destined to make an impact in this world, knowing there is more for you to be and do.

Still, there is something that has always stopped you from living your full potential and trusting yourself to "go all in." There is a secret, insecurity, or fear you just can't put your finger on. And it's not your fault. I get it that you have been searching for the truth, that is exactly what I had been searching for as well and like me everything you have tried has always missed the mark.

The insecurity or self-doubt you are secretly internalizing is "your invisible barrier." By identifying the origin of the patterns that keep you stopped, stuck, and struggling and processing the emotions tied to them will enable you the freedom to harness your innate leadership potential.

Consider that my fear of "going all in" in life began as a little girl. I was a clever kid and would soak up knowledge like a sponge and secretly knew

I was a born leader, but my fear and self-doubt would lead to overthinking and a lack of clarity which in turn, became my invisible wall. I would second guess myself, never fully trusting my capabilities.

Do you see how the law worked in my life even at that age? Even though I knew I was born to lead, when I was given the chance as school captain, the fear of going all in and stepping into my power as confident capable leader scared the sh%$ out of me.

The Law of Polarity

The second universal law that is fundamental to how life really works is the Universal Law of Polarity.

This law states that nowhere in this universe is there only a half of something existing. Simply put, everything exists in equal and opposite whole. Or another way of putting it, the law of polarity is really a law of contrast.

In practical terms, for *heat* to exist, there must be *cold* – contrast.

For *in* to exist, there must be *out* – contrast.

For *over* to exist, there must be *under* – contrast.

For a problem to exist, a solution must exist in the same moment of time!

Imagine if we never had any problems in life? I know what you are thinking!

That would be amazing, Alana, and yes, I agree, to a point.

If we never experienced problems, we would never experience the feelings of elation and accomplishment when we discover the solution, again looking at it from the perspective of contrast. I would like you to pause for a moment and consider when you are struggling with a solution to a problem, it's not that you don't always have the correct solution, it's that you don't always have the correct problem. (We will discuss this further in the next chapter.)

In this time-space continuum, in this lifetime, our greatest power is our freedom of choice, or what we might call freewill.

According to the Law of Polarity, if you were free to choose how you wanted to feel as a female business leader, what would you choose?

I know what I would choose – to feel:

- Clarity in making big decisions
- Confident in tough situations
- Powerful and poised in my communications delivery
- Compassionate and patient to those around me

And of course, because you are reading this book, you know it's not that simple.

In addition to the Universal Laws of Cause and Effect and the Law of Polarity, there is one more thing we need to explore to understand how life really works.

The human body, like all living things, is made up of atoms that have energy attached to them.

The Source, or the Divine Creator God, (universal energy) is where the energy from which we, and all life, originated from and to which we are connected to.

As humans, we were designed (or created) to be connected to this universal energy as an electric light bulb is designed to be connected to electricity.

Consider when there is a break in connection to this Divine energy source, you feel alone and disconnected from others and life, left in a whirlpool of feelings of confusion, doubt, and overwhelm.

Like an electric light without electricity, you lose your innate power.

You can feel as if you are fumbling around in the dark, searching endlessly for your true purpose, unable to reach your full potential in business and life.

For example, you might feel like you really know your stuff, that you have discovered your "zone of genius" or are in the process of discovering it, but you doubt yourself and your ability and feel like an imposter.

Maybe for you, it's feeling like you are struggling with past experiences that you are unable to let go of.

Or maybe it's feeling like you just can't be productive in the things you know you need to do.

Or that your voice isn't heard, and your decisions not acted on.

Or maybe you feel like others will judge you or you'll fail.

Sound familiar? (Me too, because I struggled with all of the above.)

Then read on!

Chapter 4

You Can't Think Your Way Out of a Feeling Problem

"The virtues of science are skepticism and independent thought."

— Walter Gilbert

This is the part of the book that starts to get really juicy and you might be thinking ...*Hmm, I'm feeling a bit skeptical about all this information, Alana* – especially if this is new to you.

That is great!

What?!

I literally mean it, that is great.

It's good to be skeptical.

Consider this, skepticism is just curiosity.

And the reason you are reading this book is because you are curious, you know there has to be a deeper reason why female leaders who are able to harness their true power to be deliberate creators of their destiny get the results they want.

They (deliberate creators) know the invisible trap they were once caught in is not a conscious, thinking problem; it is a subconscious feeling problem.

What, Alana?!

This invisible trap you are caught in is not solved by thinking your way out; it's solved from *feeling your way out*.

Stop for a moment and imagine you are about to pitch your brand to a new investor to secure a contract to take your business to the next level

Moments before this meeting occurs, you begin to feel confused, overwhelmed, and anxious. You start to doubt yourself and doubt if you even want to do this and suddenly you feel that if successful in winning the contract, this may be too big a step or too risky for your business. This fear and doubt shows up in your energy and in the way you deliver your pitch and answer their questions. You leave the meeting feeling disempowered, beating yourself up mentally, and in an almost self-fulfilling prophecy, saying to yourself, "I knew this would happen. It's easier just to stay small. I just don't have what it takes to go all in. That's for other people."

Think back to the previous chapter when I discussed the Universal Law of Polarity, that for every problem there must be a solution. According to this law, this truth, the answer to every problem is always available at any given moment in time.

And so, consider this.

You have been trying to solve the fear you hold of being a more confident and powerful leader not with the wrong solution, but with the wrong problem.

What, Alana?!

Let me explain.

If you have read books and done self-development programs, maybe even have a degree or more from a university and still don't have the results you want, then it's not that there is anything wrong with you, *and* it's not your fault.

I will repeat this and don't miss it:

It is not that there is anything wrong with you and it's not your fault! I have absolutely been there and felt exactly the same. It is because everything you have tried has missed the mark and this leaves you feeling like it must be you that is the problem.

And it is not that you haven't had the right solution (yes, that's right, I haven't made a typo).

It's just that you haven't had the right problem!

You have been trying to find a solution to a "thinking" problem, when the solution you need is for a "feeling" problem.

The problem won't get resolved from you thinking your way out. You must *feel* your way out. For example, let's explore a scenario where you are about to have a meeting to sort out an issue that has arisen with a stakeholder in your company. You want to feel confident, clear, and composed. Before the meeting, you embody the feeling of being powerful, calm, and composed by holding the intention of successfully sorting out the issue to create a win/win for you both.

You hold those feelings of confidence, composure, and power as if that end result has already happened, and the meeting has been successfully closed where both parties feel seen and heard and a win/win outcome for you both has occurred. Feeling, for how amazingly successful it all went, and how this win-win outcome will create a great outcome for further success for the company. Allowing these feelings of complete happiness and satisfaction to flood your body will activate the brain's RAS (reticular activating system). The RAS is located within the hypothalamus and brainstem and its crucial function acts as a filter to allow in essential information while tuning out unnecessary noise. Neuroscience has uncovered how important and powerful the RAS is in decision-making, productivity, and in improving a person's leadership abilities.

In addition, the RAS:

- Is the control centre for sleeping, waking, and attention
- Acts as a sophisticated filter of information
- Screens out anything it perceives as junk
- Acts as your executive assistant or high-level administrator
- Enables you to focus on what you value
- Enables you to perceive a threat
- It is the ultimate driver for intention, motivation, and productivity

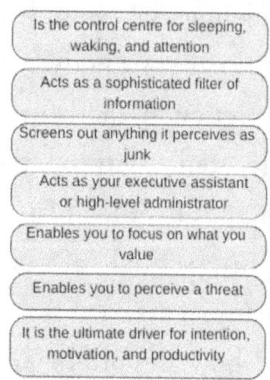
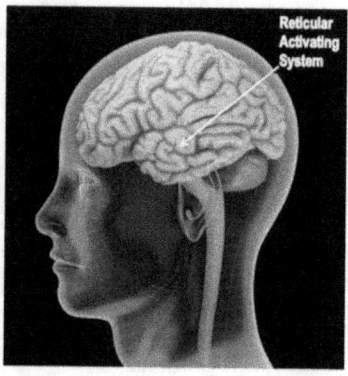

By understanding this and linking pleasure (feelings of confidence, clarity, and motivation instead of freezing in fear and self-doubt) to a situation, the mind automatically comes into alignment with those feelings and is now consciously designing or deliberately in the process of creating the desired outcome.

For example, try this exercise only if you are in a quiet place reading this book (please do not do this if you are listening to the audiobook in the car). Close your eyes for a moment and feel how your feet feel. Are they warm? Are they cold? Maybe they are neither, but the point is you can feel them; do the same with your hands. Are they warm or cold or neither?

This allows you to get out of your mind and

come back to your natural feeling state, the state we were born into.

Now feel for how you feel within your body.

If you are feeling anxious or confused, pull up and out of your mind, as if you are observing your body and how it is feeling. (This may take a little practice and focus, and it helps to focus on your breathing.)

Now choose how you would like to feel instead. Perhaps it's feeling of calm and clarity. You might feel the sense of calm in your body, perhaps in your chest or stomach, and then allow it to radiate down your arms and legs.

Acknowledge how amazing this feeling is and allow yourself just to sit in that for a minute or so until you notice clarity start to return to your mind. Stay in that feeling state for a little longer until you embody peace and calm. Your RAS will pick up this as a new state of being.

Or you may want to feel confident and capable; feel for how amazingly powerful it feels to be completely capable of anything you want to achieve.

Again, pull up and out of your mind, feeling for just how amazingly capable and powerful you are.

Embody body that feeling; it becomes a part of you (allow yourself a few minutes and yes if you are super busy you can actually do this when you take a bathroom break)I know when I want to feel like this, I feel for how easy everything is; decision-making is easy, everyday tasks are easy, and life experiences are easy. It is easy to be powerful and productive. I am capable of facing whatever I need to with ease.

Again, your RAS will pick this up as a new state of being.

Keep doing this several times a day, in the morning, afternoon, and evening before bed over the course of a week, and notice that your feelings, thoughts, belief patterns, and even your behaviours start to shift as you gain more clarity and self-confidence.

Praise yourself for these new behaviour shifts until even your daily experiences begin to show up differently. Keep celebrating yourself as *you are now awakening to your true power of being a deliberate creator and designing your reality!*

Know you have a mind, but you are not your mind. Our mind will always want to protect us or default to our protective self that was created in our earliest core trauma. Therefore, if we have run a pattern of fear and self-doubt anytime we have to lead powerfully (in business meetings for example), then that will be our default. This default pattern was caused from not having the skills to process the emotions you felt as that small child when you faced a situation that made you doubt yourself, others, and life.

This default pattern would show up particularly strongly for me when I was doing sales all those years ago, when I birthed my first business. My self-doubt would show up in my energy when selling to clients as if I somehow associated sales as being "dodgy or inauthentic." Years later, after discovering that sales are just another way of delivering amazing value to my clients, I hold a completely different attitude and energy towards it and use an "authentic selling approach." This is done by coming into alignment with my feelings, thoughts, and intentions before I physically sell my service and is ultimately achieved through embodying the feeling of how much "value" I can give to my client, knowing that my purpose in life is to create positive change and impact in the lives of female leaders. The joy that I feel in serving and empowering women to become "deliberate creators" in order to get the results they desire in business and life is incredibly fulfilling as I know I am fulfilling my life purpose.

It is so powerful for my clients to locate their earliest core trauma, and gain complete clarity on the patterns or blind spots and the emotions that have kept them trapped. The freedom and release from being able to finally process this trapped emotion and release the energy is integral in allowing them to create new positive patterns that will harness the power of the RAS.

Because, consider this, as humans we can do nothing but create, whether consciously or subconsciously. My DELIBERATE CREATOR PROCESS BY ALANA M™ is designed to awaken you to becoming a conscious creator knowing your feelings, thoughts, and intentions will in turn create your behaviours and experiences, thereby consciously shifting your reality day in and day out,

A great illustration of this is something that so many of my clients struggle with which is procrastination (which was also birthed in our earliest core trauma and usually shows up in our childhood or teenage years). I will ask them what they are consciously creating when they are procrastinating. Often, they will laugh and reply with "nothing," which I totally get; however they are actually whether consciously or subconsciously creating their procrastination.

Whether they are scrolling on social media, or watching T.V., or even comfort eating, they are actually still creating. They are creating behaviours that distract them from the task at hand which is all procrastination really is, a behaviour that distracts us from a task, right? I know it's crazy, but it's true!

And now it starts to get really exciting as we will discuss in the next chapter how you went from fearless to fearful!

Chapter 5

How You Went from Fearless to Fearful – The Power of the Subconscious Mind

"We are not afraid of things, but of how we view them."

— Epictetus

I want you to pause for a minute and think back to your earliest childhood memory. Maybe you were at a park, on a swing, or climbing in the playground – go back as early as you remember.

Just pause and take a minute. Trust that your subconscious will bring this to your conscious mind.

Are you there yet?

Good.

I guarantee in that moment of time, your young mind didn't do a risk assessment of the activity before you did it! Another way of looking at it is, you didn't overthink it. You just did it!

You also didn't spend hours of stress and worry about how proficient your climbing or swinging technique was. Meaning, even in that earliest memory, you believed you were capable of doing a task even before you had practiced or perfected it.

You had seen other children do it and you believed you could as well. Maybe not amazingly at first but you believed you could master this thing called play!

You trusted yourself. You trusted others and you trusted life!

And then something happened.

This something didn't have to feel like it was anything huge or significant but back when it happened, it was significant.

You had never had that kind of experience ever happen before and you didn't feel emotionally capable of processing it.

Much of the time this happens before age three.

What are you saying, Alana?!

I can't possibly remember what happened to me before I was three!

And the great news is that you don't have to try to work anything out, as your subconscious mind already knows!

Our minds are powerful pieces of technology and neuroscience is still figuring this out.

What is relatively less known is the power of the subconscious mind.

This is what I call the part of your consciousness as the *big* mind.

It never shuts down and is responsible for breathing and regulating your body's vital signs.

Think about it, you don't have to sit and consciously think about making your heart beat, it just does it!

The subconscious mind also stores our beliefs and values, determines our memories, and monitors the information all around us, deciding what to send to the conscious mind and what to store for later.

Another way of seeing it is that our subconscious mind is like the computer hard drive.

It stores all the information in the background that we require for life.

With that in mind, all you have to do is to ask

yourself, "What is the earliest memory I have when I felt like something happened that I never saw coming?"

This would have caused an intense amount of fear or sadness. It caused you to doubt yourself and feel like something was wrong with you and it doesn't have to be a huge trauma, although it could be It is something that affected you emotionally that you didn't expect and remember, the reason for that is because you were a little child and didn't have the emotional skills to process this emotion.

Jane's Story

As an illustration of this message, I will tell you about a client and we will call her Jane.

Jane is middle-aged and is the founder and CEO of her company. As such, she is at the forefront and is the face of her business.

She knows she is a good leader but tells me her business is at a crossroads and she needs to make some decisions to take it to the next level.

She came to me feeling stressed and burnt out.

As I sat with her and chatted, the *real* cost of the fear she internalized about her leadership ability came to the fore.

She shared with me how she would get to a certain level with her business and then fear and self-doubt would take over and the results would begin to plateau. She would then lose confidence in herself and make excuses for her business to stay small, yet she still felt unfulfilled and wanted more for both her business and her life.

This triggered a sense of failure in her. The stress from this had recently began to greatly affect not only her business but also her relationship with her partner and her children.

She was constantly feeling confused and overwhelmed unable to make effective decisions making her impatient and irritable to those around her, including her friends and family.

She felt unable to ask for the help she needed from her team and her business partner and would often hide away in an effort to self-soothe rather than self-acknowledge and make her needs known.

She had often struggled with overthinking and procrastination. This was becoming steadily worse, which only added to her stress.

I asked if she could share a little about her childhood.

She had shared that as a child she was shy and never really enjoyed being in the limelight.

She had suffered from anxiety for most of her adult life with it becoming increasingly worse with age.

She had tried meditation, breath work, positive affirmations, and reframing, and even though these would help she still felt there was something else missing that she couldn't put her finger on. As if there was something more that was stopping her from stepping into her true power to get the results she wanted.

She never understood the *real* reason why she seemed to reach a certain level of success in business and then either self-sabotage her results or freeze and feel unable to go any further.

She had just resigned herself to thinking that something must be wrong with her.

I began by sharing my story with her and then explaining to her how life really works according to the Universal Law of Cause and Effect and the Universal Law of Polarity.

Like me, she also shared that she felt exhausted from trying to control everything and everyone in life. Caught in the trap of constantly "trying to control" and feeling like she could never really control anything left her frustrated, tired and disengaged.

As we began working together, I asked what her childhood had been like. She had grown up in a good home with parents who, like her, had operated their own business

She told me she didn't recall having anything traumatic happen. I went on to tell her that a core trauma does not have to be anything huge. It is similar to the old saying, "it is in the eye of the beholder."

However, after I started guiding her back to her early childhood using Step 2 of my DELIBERATE CREATOR PROCESS BY ALANA M™ I asked her to *feel* for a time in her earliest memory when she felt like she trusted herself, she trusted others, and she trusted life. A memory of her wearing a blue Cinderella dress emerged.

She shared that she had loved dressing up, as most little girls do, and she recalled she had felt so pretty and special in that dress.

As the moments assed, I noticed a frowned, sad expression start to emerge across her face.

I encouraged her to tell me where this feeling was coming from.

She went on to tell me she was recalling one occasion.

She was wearing the same Cinderella dress,

this time with make-up on her face, eyeshadow spilling out over her eyelids and onto her cheek bones.

There was lipstick smeared across her lips in a messy, almost clown-like application, just like any toddler would when applying it themselves.

I asked if she knew how old she was. Jane thought around two years old.

I asked her to feel for what happened next.

After a long pause, she told me she could visualise herself dancing and twirling in the hallway, and she knew it was the house they used to live in at that time. I reassured and encouraged her, telling her how well she was doing in recalling this from her subconscious.

I asked her to feel for what happened next.

She went on to say she senses she goes into the kitchen where her mother was preparing dinner.

She told me her mother turned around from the kitchen bench.

After a long pause, emotion overwhelmed Jane and with tears rolling down her cheeks; Jane went on to tell me she knew her mother was yelling as her.

She told me she knew her mum was furious at

her and is yelling at her for getting into her make-up.

I sat with her as she processed and released the emotional energy that had been stored in her body for the last forty-five years.

Jane went on to tell me she didn't remember much of anything else that evening.

She just remembered becoming a shy, nervous child.

She had always loved ballet but choose team sports at school instead for fear of performing in front of people alone.

As we discussed her experience, I went onto tell her that that was *her earliest core trauma.*

Up until that point, Jane had trusted herself, trusted others, and trusted life.

She knew she had felt capable of this thing called life even before she knew what it really involved.

Until that one moment when she felt blindsided by that experience as a two-year-old child who didn't have the skills to process her emotions.

I asked her the question, "What did that little girl, that two-year-old Jane make it mean about herself, life, and others?"

Again, with raw emotion, Jane went on to say that she made it mean that:

- Real fulfillment was unattainable
- Making decisions was hard, as she was constantly overthinking and second-guessing, so it was easier just to procrastinate
- Asking for help was a sign of weakness
- Showing up as a powerful female leader would mean judgement and failure

Jane never saw this one core trauma experience as the pivotal point in her life that led to the birth of her protective self or ego, that created her "invisible wall."

That one experience was the catalyst for the pattern or programming she had subconsciously run the majority of her life which made her unable to trust herself, trust others, and trust life.

Her earliest core trauma meant she had created a perception or a belief about herself and life that had held her captive for the majority of her life with feelings of fear, anxiety and self-doubt.

And I asked her to consider that a perception or a belief is just that, a perception or a belief.

But is it the truth?

In actual fact, a perception or belief about ourselves, others, and life is just a habit or thought we keep thinking.

I went onto explain to Jane that in no way was I trying to diminish what she had been feeling about herself for most of her life; instead, I asked her to consider that if it was true that real fulfillment was unattainable, that would mean that real fulfillment was unattainable for everyone, and that's not necessarily true.

For it to be true that making decisions meant overthinking and second-guessing, must mean making decisions involves overthinking and second guessing for everyone and that is not necessarily the case.

For it to be true that asking for help was a sign of weakness, it must mean that everyone perceives asking for help is a weakness, and again, that is not necessarily true.

For it to mean showing up as a powerful female leader would mean judgement and failure, must mean that's true for every female leader, and that's not necessarily so. (See Chapter 9).

Again, I went on to assure her it was not her fault, and this was not about morality (right or wrong). I was simply using this to illustrate contrast, and according to the Universal Law of Polarity, the opposite must exist in any given solution. This would be the "gold" that Jane had been searching for.

Now that we had located the real reason for her self-sabotaging thought patterns (blind spots) that had been birthed in her earliest core trauma, we could process the trapped emotion for her to return to her true self, to harness her innate power to be the confident, powerful leader she was destined to be. This was the secret to shattering the invisible barrier that had been holding her business back. Finally, she could find real mental clarity and emotional and financial freedom.

I went on to explain to her that we really can't separate business from life, the patterns we run will show up in all areas of our lives, including our relationships whether personal or professional, and the daily choices and decisions we make on a personal and professional basis. And I explained that business is really just about communication in creating win/win relationships. Ultimately having successful professional relationships with our clients, employees, and business partners with the intention that both parties feel they are in a win/win situation.

We must hold the higher intention of entering into any communication with the desire of achieving the best outcome possible for each party and not necessarily what will benefit only one side. As this higher intention is held and embodied as a state of being with the actions that follow, according to the universal laws, our results must show up accordingly. Again, this is not about right or wrong, it is just how the laws operate.

As an illustration, imagine you have a team member or business partner who is struggling to meet deadlines and you need to address the issue in a meeting. Pull up and out of your mind and feel for how you want the meeting to go. Know you want to communicate with clarity, staying in your power. Feel for the outcome, the win /win situation for you, your team members, and ultimately the productivity of your business.

In practical terms, you might approach the meeting with something like this.

First, form a rapport and let the team member /business partner know this is a safe space for her to speak anything on her mind.

Second, allow her to be seen and heard by acknowledging (I didn't say agreeing to) the reason / reasons for her missed deadlines. Imagine that you are emptying a cup full of water as you are present and hear her; in this case, the reason(s) is the water in the cup. Once you have heard and acknowledged the reason(s), the cup will be empty. This means the person feels seen and heard and the mind is free to be present to process the information that follows.

Next, discuss the "bigger picture" outcome of how important deadlines are for the success of the business and the importance of you both being in alignment (agreement) with this.

What is her part in that?

What your part is in that?

This is the beginning of forming a conscious agreement.

It involves both parties collaborating keeping, the big picture in mind.

For example, you might offer her further support and accountability.

In exchange, ask for her to think of three strategies that she could implement to overcome her lack of consistency in keeping deadlines.

Identify in advance any obstacles that might

occur that would get in the way of a successful resolution.

Finally, know it is not enough just to form a new agreement moving forward, as each person has to agree on what new behaviours have to be applied as a habit for success to occur. A great practical example of this is identifying what has to change on each of your calendars to make this happen and by when.

The best agreement between two parties is what is called a "conscious agreement."

This goes deeper than just agreeing on meeting an expectation by identifying new behaviours or actions and a time frame when this will happen.

In other words, we have each consciously made it.

Further, we have each agreed upon the behaviours or actions necessary and by when those behaviours or actions will happen. This means we both see the win/win by aligning with the bigger purpose.

A common blindspot that can happen in business is forming an agreement with the acumen it never has to be altered. In the business world this is just not reality which is why to create success, a culture that promotes a safe space to raise issues and renegotiate agreements should be fostered,

Back to Jane — now that she uncovered the reason for the patterns she ran that affected her on a business level, the next step was to support her in fully processing her emotions, freeing her to step into her true power to deliberately design and create her destiny This would allow Jane to work within these laws so she could create the results she desired with ease and flow instead of feeling stopped, stuck, and struggling.

In the next chapter, we will look at the difference between the protective self that was created from our earliest core trauma and our true self, from where we can become a deliberate creator and design the impact we are here to make.

Chapter 6

The False Self vs. the True Self

"The ego is only an illusion, but a very influential one."

— Wayne Dyer

As humans, our greatest desire is to be seen and heard. When my three daughters were little, they would naturally want all my attention, as all children do. One of my girls was particularly curious and very active.

This meant it was always a juggle to keep all three entertained and being indoors meant boredom and the inability to run around would often produce fights between them.

As any mum knows, young kids need time

playing every day. When things became all too much and I thought I might lose my sanity, I would send them outdoors into the backyard to play.

Two win-wins occurred from this – one, they got to burn off energy and two, I could get things done without becoming completely deranged from the chaos.

My daughter who was curious and active was also adventurous and our current home at the time had a rainwater tank in the backyard.

She would climb up onto the external air conditioning unit, wrap her body around the external downpipe that connected to the tank, climb on top of the water tank, and jump off.

And yes, she is fine to this day with no adverse effects.

Since she couldn't be seen and heard in the house, she soon got my attention after a couple of attempts of this adventurous feat.

I tell this to further illustrate Jane's story.

At the very core of Jane's being, she desired to be seen and heard, but the unprocessed emotions she held from her core trauma meant she stayed small and internalized her fear and self-doubt. She could now see her coping mechanism was to hide away in an effort to self-soothe and this would only make her anxiety and self-doubt worse.

Even though she knew she was intelligent and a natural leader and wanted to go all in to achieve the results she had always dreamed of for her company, fear and self-doubt would take her out (her invisible barrier).

Jane continued through life feeling like something was wrong with her.

As a result of this trauma, her subconscious mind had formed a protective self (or false self) to survive life. This meant that she was constantly "in her head" trying to use logic to "fix herself or her way of thinking." Of course no amount of logic could ever "fix" what Jane had thought was wrong with her. In essence, there was actually nothing wrong with her as she had been constantly operating from her "protective self" in order to just survive life. She would soon discover that her lack of capability was only a perception in her mind, albeit a very real perception that had kept her trapped for the majority of her life.

Jane's true self, the true Jane was exactly who she was created to be, fully capable, completely powerful possessing amazing clarity in all areas of her life. She would soon know this as not just as a concept but as a living, breathing embodiment when she could separate the truth from the lies to return to alignment or to her "true self."

Remember our subconscious is not concerned about morality (right or wrong) or truth or lie but instead will run patterns that will help to protect us or help us to "survive" life.

With this pattern continually running, she felt locked in an invisible trap from which she could never escape. I explained to her that when we are constantly in our mind when making decisions, our big-picture view of things becomes distorted and we often end up overthinking which leads to confusion, overwhelm, and exhaustion. We are born with a natural feeling state which we know as our "gut" or intuition. Young children are very good at connecting with their intuition and many of us lose this as we get older.

Another way we lose this connection is from our earliest core trauma, when we yet don't have the skills to process our emotion and thus lose trust in our innate ability to feel and decide intuitively.

Hence Jane had made a subconscious decision she couldn't trust *herself* to get the results she truly desired in business and life.

She had made a subconscious decision she couldn't trust *others*, as they would judge her.

She had made a subconscious decision she couldn't trust *life*.

These subconscious feelings of mistrust then became her beliefs.

Her beliefs became her behaviours. Her behaviours then became her experiences.

Her experiences showed up in the results she did or didn't get.

As we continued to meet together, I helped to guide her back to her core trauma but this time observing the experience as a bystander.

I worked with her to separate the truth from the lies so she could return to alignment, Step 3 in my process. These were the blind spots that that kept her trapped in her perception of herself, others, and life.

The first thing she observed that she had made a lie was the perception that there was something wrong with her.

She felt for the truth, because what she thought was reality, was a perception she had formed, therefore a lie. She had just been a curious little girl who believed she was capable of anything.

The next misconception (lie) Jane had created

from her earliest core trauma was that to show up as a powerful, confident leader would mean judgement and failure.

I asked her to feel for the truth of what happened that day as a two-year-old in front of her mum.

She told me she saw that her mother reacted in the moment after a busy, stressful day as any mother would if their child had gotten into make-up. Except, as a little child, she could never have seen this coming and her young mind did not have the skills to fully process the emotion that accompanied this.

The truth was that she knew she was a born leader, capable of being confident and powerful as she had been the CEO of her company for the last seven years.

The next lie she felt for was the perception that she couldn't trust herself to make big decisions in business and life (which was the root cause of her procrastination). Another way of hearing this was she had linked pain and fatigue to decision-making and getting big tasks and projects done which naturally meant she delayed doing these things.

As an observer of her experience, she said that in her excitement she caught her mother off guard and her mother reacted from her anger of Jane getting into her make-up. Because the two-year-old Jane did not have the skillsets to process her emotions, her protective self made it mean to make decisions was exhausting and hard and ultimately risked judgement and failure. and This was the real reason that she struggled with decision-making and procrastination.

That didn't mean Jane couldn't be trusted, as her business partner and team trusted her daily to lead and make decisions. And I explained to her that each time she made a decision to link massive pleasure to it as the RAS will pick this up as a new way of being. Now she had uncovered her true self, decision making would become easier as she would experience clarity instead of confusion and overwhelm.

As Jane built back trust and confidence in herself, she went on to say that the beliefs she had created about not trusting others or life couldn't be true. I continued to assure her it wasn't her fault for believing these lies, as they were created subconsciously from her earliest core trauma as a form of protection.

She paused for a long time and then laughed, "This is crazy!"

These were the blind spots, the lies that had kept her bound in her invisible trap for so long. By exposing these, her invisible barrier now became visible.

She asked me how she didn't see it sooner.

I smiled and explained to her that it was because we *can't see our own blind spots* which is why they are blind spots!

This is akin to the old saying, "You can't see the forest for the trees."

And that is the exact reason why we stay trapped in the self-sabotaging cycle of hitting an invisible barrier, unable to achieve the outcomes we crave in business and life.

I explained to her that everything in life is about timing. Human nature is the same in every race and nation of people. Consider this, from the moment we are born, we are taught to become independent, which is great life skill, but it is also a double-edged sword. Of course, independence is a trait every mother wants for her child but often our subconscious mind will then associate *asking for help* as a perceived weakness or should I say a perception of perceived weakness.

And considering what we have discussed previously, is a perception truth? I was the world's worst at asking for help. I would quietly resent the fact I wanted help but wouldn't allow myself to ask for it until the frustration turned to anger and I would explode in front of those around me (and I know you as the reader can probably resonate). I would state my case that I had no support in a project or decision, when I hadn't even asked for it in the first place! Yes, I used to expect everyone around me to be mind readers and act accordingly. Sound familiar? This was a big blind spot or behaviour pattern for me, even though in hindsight I secretly knew I was doing it.

And the secret to uncovering and solving the real reason for our blind spots is found in our subconscious mind that were created from our earliest core trauma. Once uncovered, these blind spots (misconceptions) can be cleared. Then we are finally free to step into our true leadership power, to be the deliberate creators we were always destined to be, to get the results we have always craved.

In the next chapter, we will discuss what we need to put down to become a deliberate creator and shape your destiny!

Chapter 7

What You Need to Give up to Be a "Deliberate Creator"

"The only real battle in life is between hanging on and letting go."

— Shannon L. Alder

In Chapter 3, I discussed how I had felt separate for almost as long as I could remember. I felt alone and disconnected from others and life, and I didn't feel like I belonged or fitted in anywhere.

I had a strong will, which meant I was a driven leader. I also felt my life was constantly out of control and tried mercilessly to control whatever I could about myself and others, only to feel exhausted and powerless.

If this sounds familiar, you know you are not alone, and I'm going to say something now that you feel might like you already know.

To be the deliberate creator of your life, you have to put down the need to control. I get it, I really do that this is huge, and it isn't easy! And guess what, every single person on this planet struggles with this and if they say they don't, they aren't being truthful to themselves. I know this because I absolutely was one of those people!

And I need you to look lovingly with curiosity and no judgement as you consider that this need originated from the protective self that was created from your earliest core trauma and the protective self *can't do anything else but control*. Consider, when you had that one event happen as a child that you never saw coming, and you didn't have the skills to process your emotion, the protective self created the need to control in order for you to feel safe and secure.

I want you to look at the need to control (others, situations, and life in general) as an observer, like Jane did in her earliest core trauma.

Get curious, and without any judgement towards yourself, ask yourself these three questions:

1. Where has that need to control come from?
2. Can I really control anything in life?
3. How can I stop the need for being in control?

I will answer the above questions in the order I gave them.

1. The need for control comes from the false (protective) self and was created from your earliest core trauma. Such was the intensity of the emotion that you were unable to process as a little child, which in turn created your blind spots or misconceptions about yourself, others, and life. To protect yourself from further hurt (trauma), you subconsciously choose to control instead.
2. The illusion of control is just that, an illusion, which is the reason why you feel confused, overwhelmed, unfulfilled, and burnt out from trying to attain something, which will always be beyond your grasp.

3. This is the answer to the million-dollar question and here it is: just put it down. I mean that with love and complete sincerity, to step into your true power, you have to put down the need to control.

And to this end I want you to consider that until your earliest core trauma is uncovered along with the blind spots that accompany it, you will always have the need to control. That is why you can't break free from this self-sabotaging cycle, that invisible barrier that is robbing you of your true power, your true potential, and the results you desire.

Once I guide you to uncover both your earliest core trauma and the blind spots that your subconscious mind has stored away for the majority of your life, you are free to fully process the trapped emotion (Step 3), returning to alignment *or* true self.

From alignment, you are then able to create a "vivid vision" for your business and life. This is a living, breathing vision that is not just a "concept" but something that is embodied day in and day out discussed in my trademarked methodology.

It is worth noting that in the past you may have created a vision for your life, but it never quite became a reality. This is because a vision is an awareness of a concept. However, just having an awareness is not enough to get you a result. A "vivid vision" is something that is not only designed but embodied as if you are already living it, practically applying the skills, the subtle changes in thoughts, intentions and actions day in and day out until the vision shows up as reality. This is exactly why I developed my DELIBERATE CREATOR PROCESS BY ALANA M™ methodology. It is a process that not only supports you in designing a vision but delivers you the necessary skillsets to deliberately make that vision a reality.(Step 4).

Through my customized plan and succinct methodology, you will finally be able to put down the need to control. I will show you how to return to alignment (true self) and work within the universal laws to harness your innate leadership power to be the deliberate creator of your business and your life, finally finding the fulfillment you crave. When we work with these laws and not against them, the real magic happens. It's like swimming with the current and not against it!

Think back to my story of that day in court. I knew I had no control over what my ex-husband's barrister was going to do or say. I had no control over the questions she was going to ask me or the manner in which she delivered them. I had no control over which judge was to be hearing the case that day. I had no control over the judge's thoughts or how he would view my case.

I had to put down my perception that I could really control anything. This was achieved by returning to alignment or my true self (Step 3). It was only once this was done that I could step into my true power to become a conscious, deliberate creator.

As the date for the hearing drew near, I held the intention that my case was already won, and embodied that feeling through my whole body, knowing that after five years it would finally be over. Knowing how amazing this felt and visualizing it as already won simply meant I had to hold this intention until it became reality. This was achieved through my words and actions in court that day, knowing that the results would inevitably follow. This was the secret to how I was able to answer every question with absolute clarity and confidence and not get taken out of my power.

And according to the Law of Cause and Effect, the results followed as they must.

From that moment on, I began fully living this truth in every area of my life. The shy ten-year-old schoolgirl (my protective self) became the deliberate and conscious creator of my destiny using my own trademarked methodology and stepped into her true leadership power and potential.

My ultimate purpose is to empower and serve women like you who are reading this book to do the same by uncovering truth:

- Step 1: The truth about how life really works
- Step 2: The truth how you became disconnected from your power and the self-sabotaging patterns that run as a result of this
- Step 3: The truth of how returning to alignment (your true self) will enable you to step into your true power
- Step 4: The truth about creating a "vivid vision" as a living breathing vision is more than just a concept
- Step 5: The truth of when the correct skillsets are applied to that vision you

will get the outcome you desire
- Step 6: The truth that life is really for you, and you can actually find real joy and fulfillment in the journey of living as the deliberate creator of your destiny!

Chapter 8

The Secret to True Power and Freedom

"The most powerful weapon on earth is the human soul on fire!"

— Ferdinand Foch

Consider how amazingly capable we all were at just about anything as a young child.

Consider how you went from crawling to walking.

You could never crawl fast enough to walk.

And consider this, you never read a book or instruction manual on how you could go from crawling to walking.

In essence, you needed a "quantum leap" to go

to your next developmental stage *and that's exactly what happened!*

Your subconscious mind just knew what to do. You didn't do a risk assessment of the activity before you did it. Sure, you probably sucked at it at first and had the bumps and bruises to prove it, but subconsciously you trusted you were *capable* of doing it!

As I continued working with Jane, I asked her if she was ready to forgive herself for believing these lies that she had created from her core trauma as truth knowing that it wasn't her fault. After all, true power and freedom to actually live our destiny lies in the power of choice.

She agreed and chose to forgive herself.

This one decision (choice) gave her a tremendous sense of power and freedom.

I asked her to consider that the truth is that we only ever feel as confident to the level that we feel we are capable. *And we will only ever get the level of results in life as to the level of how capable we feel.*

I explained to her that on average, over 90 percent of the time our thoughts are coming from our subconscious programming, which dictates our feelings, our behaviours and our experiences, which ultimately dictates our results. In addition, 20 percent of our efforts will produce 80 percent of our results. Consider what we focus on and the intentions we create will be the energy we hold, which will ultimately show up in our behaviours and actions which is the key to achieving the results we desire.

When we believe we are truly capable, we shift reality of how we see ourselves, others, and life. This is the secret to the "quantum leap" that is required to close the gap from where we are to where we want to be in business and life.

The truth is that we are capable, we were born to be capable, and the real power lies in the freedom to choose to awaken and harness that power.

Once we feel for the truth in trusting we are fully capable of being confident and powerful, it will show up in our new feelings, thoughts, behaviours, and experiences, and we will achieve the results we desire.

As I once again shared with Jane the story of that day in court, the day I chose to be fully capable and "went all in" to achieve the results I desired using my trademarked methodology DELIBERATE CREATOR PROCESS BY

ALANA M™, I asked her if she was ready to decide that she was capable of taking her company to the next level, to awaken to her true leadership power and potential.

This time, it would be different as she had put down the need to control and had chosen to step into her true power to intentionally shift her feelings, thoughts, behaviours, and actions to create new experiences leading to new results, ultimately being the deliberate creator of her life.

In feeling for the answer, she agreed she was *all in* in creating the results she desired by working within the universal laws which would allow her to create with ease and flow, instead of trying to control, bringing with it confusion, frustration, overwhelm, and exhaustion.

We worked together to create *"a vivid vision"* a *living, breathing outcome* of what success for her company and ultimately her life would look like moving forward giving her amazing clarity for the exact results she wanted to create. From there I ensured she had a *customized plan* to follow to close the gap from where she was to where she wanted to be.

Over the sessions that followed, I continued to coach her in the new skillsets to take her confidence and communication and leadership skills to the next level (Step 5).

I asked Jane to consider that communication is both a talent and a skill that can be learned so she would feel confident to have difficult conversations without ever losing her power.

Indeed, it is possible to have tough conversations, even if there has been a difference of opinion or a disagreement:

- Without always agreeing or people pleasing
- Without going into defensive mode, blaming, or shaming the other person
- Whether you're the leader, or team member

And it is absolutely possible for any leader to master this!

Knowing that before she entered into difficult conversations, there were a few things Jane was going to have to let go of first, including:

- The need to always be right (which stems from the protective self or ego that never wants to be seen as wrong)

- Fear of being judged (again protective self)
- Thinking that there is only "one right way" where there may be other efficient ways to do things
- Taking it personally (when someone disagrees with you, it doesn't necessarily mean they are intentionally against you or don't like you, as it could simply mean they have a difference of opinion)

Feeling for the truth, I asked her to consider that in order for successful communication to happen all that is required is the willingness and frankness of two people's minds to join in communion.

Additionally, I explained that we can't hold on to a position (that is to always be right) and be willing to communicate at the same time.

I went on to say that initially, all it takes is at least one person who is willing to let go of their position and model this, consistently, for business partners and team members to follow this lead to achieve success for the greater whole.

I explained to Jane, that along with our

blindspots, there are often *money blocks* that have been subconsciously created (e.g. that she was undeserving of having the wealth she desired) from her earliest core trauma. Once these are located and removed, there would be nothing to hold her back from completely shattering the barrier holding her business back.

For Jane, true fulfillment and success looked something like the following:

- From self-doubt to self-confidence
- From procrastination to motivation
- From confusion to clarity when communicating and decision-making
- From feeling stressed and burnt out to feeling a sense of true power (calm)
- From frustration and overwhelm to peace and alignment
- From undeserving to worthy of the wealth she desired

This finally allowing her to experience real joy and fulfillment in her work, relationships, and life.

From then on, she could confidently and intentionally shift her reality day in and day out to deliberately design and live her destiny to get the results she had always desired.

I know you are reading this and are thinking in the same vein as the iconic line from *When Harry Met Sally* – "I'll have what she (Jane) is having!" And you absolutely can! You are more capable than you know and because you have read this far in *Breakthrough to Entrepreneurial Brilliance,* you have awakened to the truth that life can be really for you and not against you when you understand how life really works.

This is the truth I know you have been searching for such a long time! Feel for just how powerful and capable you are! Embody that feeling of power, clarity, and calm until it becomes a part of you, then praise, praise, praise yourself because you have just taken the first step to being a deliberate creator of your reality.

You are actually doing this, consciously (deliberately) designing and shifting your reality in the small things that will ultimately create change in your feelings, thoughts, and behaviours, which will affect your experiences, day in and day out until the results you desire begin to materialize.

Chapter 9

For Such a Time as This (From the Ancient Hebrew Book of Esther)

"The secret of change is to focus all of your energy not on fighting the old, but on building the new."

— Socrates

In the Old Testament scriptures (Bible) there is quite a remarkable book about a beautiful young queen called Esther.

This powerful story from the ancient history of the Hebrews (Jews), tells of a young woman who stands face to face against an empire who is on the verge of complete genocide of her people, the ancient Hebrews who we now know as the Jewish race. If this plot is to succeed, then not only would

Esther and her family be killed, but the entire Jewish race would also cease to exist.

Esther, who was orphaned as a child, was adopted by a Jewish family. As a young woman, she is chosen to be a member of the Persian King Ahasuerus's harem.

She immediately is noticed by the king for her beauty and is crowned queen. As with any good story, there must be a villain (let's say narcissist) who is more concerned with his own power and illusion of control than anything else. The story of Esther is no different.

After corruption in the king's camp, a new military officer called Haman is appointed to be the king's right-hand man. The power quickly goes to Haman's head, and he orders every citizen in the kingdom to bow down and worship him not only whenever anyone is in his company but also as he passes by. Esther's family refuses to worship this evil man.

As the story unfolds, we find Haman, furious with this family for not doing as he commands, true to character issuing a vendetta not only against Esther's family, but against the whole Jewish race. He issues an edict that every Jew be hanged.

Esther has one and only chance to save her

family and her people from certain genocide from the Persian Empire. Believing she can persuade King Ahasuerus to overturn this edict and open his eyes to see just how evil Haman really is, she accepts the challenge.

As you read the book of Esther, you will discover that there is a Divine force that permeates each scene.

Nothing is truly coincidental, and even though we know little about her, we imagine Esther as a confident, powerful young woman who knows she is completely capable of saving an entire race of people from extinction. She accepts the challenge and chooses to awaken to her true power and becomes the leader she was always destined to be.

When things seem to be looking the worst for Queen Esther and her people, when evil looks as if it will win, Esther steps forward. Harnessing the universal power of an unseen source, she harnesses her true leadership power and becomes a deliberate designer of her destiny', ultimately creating the results she desires. This was her time to create a global impact and as such she will be known throughout history as the saviour of a nation – "For such a time as this." (Esther 4:14 NIV)

In so doing (spoiler alert if you want to check

this story out) the evil Haman meets a well-deserved fate and the Jewish people triumph.

Why am I telling you this story?

Quite simply, there have been so many amazing women throughout history who have been remembered for the way in which they have impacted and shaped our world.

Who comes to mind for you?

For me it's Malala Yousafzai, the young Pakistani girl, who on October 9, 2012 whilst taking the bus home from school, was shot in an assignation attempt by a Taliban gunman.

She had been targeted as an activist for female education. Not only did she survive but this only made her become more fearless in her pursuit for every girl to have a right to an education. She went on to win the Nobel Peace Prize in 2014.

What an incredible leader, spokeswoman, and change-maker this young woman is for women's rights globally!

The women who we identify with as powerful global leaders already knew the secrets contained in this book.

They also knew it was their time!

They knew they were born leaders and

believed their time on this earth was for a definite reason, a greater purpose.

If they hadn't become "deliberate creators" and created their destiny, things would be different in two ways:

1. They would have never realized just how powerful they were
2. The world would have been a much darker place without them (consider the story of Queen Esther and Malala Yousafzai)

So too this is your time – you are a born leader, and you are on this planet at this particular time in history or bigger things! You are destined for a greater purpose. I believe this with all of my heart, and I hope and pray that the words on these pages have empowered you to believe in yourself with a renewed passion.

My message to you is the same message I received in my dream so many years ago, "Get up, straighten your crown, and become all you were destined to be!"

You are more capable than you know and like

me, you can be the deliberate creator of your business, your life, and your destiny, and find real joy and fulfillment in the process. You will experience the process as more than just a concept and get the results you have always wanted, mental clarity and emotional and financial freedom.

Afterword

As we bring this book in for landing, I know you are reading this because you want to break through to entrepreneurial brilliance. You have always had a desire to make a greater impact and find mental clarity, fulfillment, and emotional and financial freedom.

You've always known this and yet something is still missing in your search for fulfillment.

You also feel like something must be wrong with you because you haven't been able to step into your full leadership potential to get the results you want in business and life.

You feel stuck in an invisible trap, disempowered and exhausted from trying to manage and control everything.

Afterword

Your deepest desire is to discover and live your destiny. Or conversely you may already know what you want you are destined to do, and the impact you want to make but you don't know how to make it a reality.

You feel powerless in situations with certain personality types like that one prickly client, business partner, or team leader.

You struggle to find clarity when making business and life decisions.

Your deepest desire is to trust yourself to feel completely capable of getting the results you desire.

You have tried before (maybe many times) to close the gap from where you are to where you want to be but have never got the results you know you are meant for.

Consider this – I would love you to consider it is not by chance you purchased this book and now is the time to for you to awaken to your true power. I have journeyed with and empowered women just like you who are passionate for truth knowing they are destined for greater impact. They have so much to give but struggle with *fully* trusting their leadership capabilities to get the results they desire in business and life.

Afterword

Through my trademarked methodology you can become a deliberate creator of your destiny as more than just a concept, but truly live it in reality. As you awaken to your *true* power your vision will stop being "just a concept" as I walk alongside you to help make it "become a reality" to experience the mental clarity and emotional and financial freedom you are searching for.

As you work within the truth of the Universal Laws and the methodology discussed in this book, you will experience how to a create your results with ease and flow instead of fear and doubt, finding real joy and fulfillment in the process

It's a simple six-step recipe that we have discussed throughout the pages in this book with my **DELIBERATE CREATOR PROCESS BY ALANA M**™ that is customized to close the gap from where you are to where you want to be, getting you results in the shortest possible time- saving you a fortune in time, stress and money.

You are the deliberate creator of your business, your life, and ultimately your destiny.

You already have this power, it just needs to be re-awakened in you!

Much love and blessings,

Alana

Afterword

Connect with me to create your own complimentary, customized plan for breakthrough via alana@breakthoughtobrilliancebook.com.au!

Acknowledgments

To my dad, who taught me to be resilient.

To my mum, who always believed in and supported me.

To my brother, for his unique sense of humour, "says it like it is," has amazing determination and a heart of gold.

To my three daughters, Hannah, Katie and Chloe, you are and will always be my greatest joy!

To my beautiful friend Hayley, for always being in my corner. You are my biggest cheerleader.

To my ex-husband for providing for me a life of contrast so I could learn to discover who I really was.

Like you, I am on this journey of life, and what an exciting journey it is. Knowing we were all designed to be connected to the ultimate deliberate creator, God, to be the deliberate creator of our destiny is incredibly freeing. Understanding we have the power of choice to create our reality newly day in and day out. May you have the courage to come home to who you were destined to be! Confident, courageous, with complete clarity in who you are, unleashing your potential to the world.

To my partner, Tom. Thank you for always believing in me and allowing me the opportunity to be me.

And finally, to all my clients, thank you for trusting me to journey with you through your deepest life experiences. Thank you for having the courage to break through that invisible barrier to be the deliberate creator of your life.

You will always encourage and inspire me.

Abundant blessings!

About the Author

Alana Mills is a life transformation expert, an intuitive spiritual healer, international best-selling author, sought-after motivational speaker, internationally qualified fitness and wellness coach, and a mum of three incredible daughters.

After years of feeling like she was hitting an invisible wall in business and life, she became the deliberate creator of her destiny. Putting down the need to control and micromanage, she awakened and stepped into her true power.

As an intuitive spiritual healer, Alana is able to free you from fear, doubt, and anxiety by guiding you to locate your earliest core trauma to identify your blind spots. This allows you to fully process your emotions to return to your true power, enabling you to find mental clarity, emotional fulfillment and financial freedom to get the results you have always desired in business and life.

Alana developed her trademarked methodology specifically for female coaches, leaders and entrepreneurs and works with them to design and live their destiny. DELIBERATE CREATOR PROCESS BY ALANA M™ is the process that enables healing and transformation, ultimately empowering them to *live* the life they were destined for, making the impact they were meant to make.

Alana is passionate about revealing the secrets that are the game changers between knowing your potential and actually living it. This is achieved by combining the emotional, physical, and spiritual awareness to operate from balance and harmony, with ease and flow.

She now lives her full potential, being the deliberate designer and creator of her destiny with her partner Tom, her three daughters and their French bulldog Bambam. She currently lives in Brisbane, Queensland, Australia and loves fitness, running, reading and great coffee!

About Difference Press

Difference Press is the publishing arm of The Author Incubator, an Inc. 500 award-winning company that helps business owners and executives grow their brand, establish thought leadership, and get customers, clients, and highly-paid speaking opportunities, through writing and publishing books.

While traditional publishers require that you already have a large following to guarantee they make money from sales to your existing list, our approach is focused on using a book to grow your following – even if you currently don't have a following. This is why we charge an up-front fee but never take a percentage of revenue you earn from your book.

☞ More than a Coach. More than a Publisher. ✍

We work intimately and personally with each of our authors to develop a revenue-generating strategy for the book. By using a Lean Startup style methodology, we guarantee the book's success before we even start writing. We provide all the technical support authors need with editing, design, marketing, and publishing, the emotional support you would get from a book coach to help you manage anxiety and time constraints, and we serve as a strategic thought partner engineering the book for success.

The Author Incubator has helped almost 2,000 entrepreneurs write, publish, and promote their non-fiction books. Our authors have used their books to gain international media exposure, build a brand and marketing following, get lucrative speaking engagements, raise awareness of their product or service, and attract clients and customers.

☞ Are you ready to write a book? ✍

As a client, we will work with you to make sure your book gets done right and that it gets done quickly. The Author Incubator provides one-stop for strategic book consultation, author coaching to manage writer's block and anxiety, full-service professional editing, design, and self-publishing services, and book marketing and launch campaigns. We sell this as one package so our clients are not slowed down with contradictory advice. We have a 99 percent success rate with nearly all of our clients completing their books, publishing them, and reaching bestseller status upon launch.

☞ Apply Now and Be Our Next Success Story ✍

To find out if there is a significant ROI for you, get on our calendar by completing an application at www.TheAuthorIncubator.com/apply.

Other Books by Difference Press

Fundraising without Burnout: Radically Reimagining Philanthropy to Transform Your Impact by Radha Friedman

22 Millionaire Money Codes: Create a 7-Figure Legacy Business as a Real Estate Professional by Connie Grant

Art of the Heart: The Doctor-Patient Partnership by Jay H. Kleiman, MD

Living Intentionally after Loss: 8 Steps to Reclaiming Your Passion and Purpose by Maya Manseau

Is This a Cult?: Confronting the Line between Transformation and Exploitation by Anne. L. Peterson

Prove Them Wrong: One Immigrant's 10-Year Journey from Bankrupt to Millionaire by Héctor E. Quiroga, J.D.

Build a Business with Gusto: Attracting Strategic Investors to Fund Your Vision by Greg Weiss

Swipe Right, Laugh Hard: Online Dating Adventures for the Woman Who's Given Up by Juli A. Wills

Thank You!

"We are all here for some special reason. Stop being the prisoner of your past. Become the architect of your future."

— Robin Sharma

Thank you! I feel so much joy and appreciation that you have read this book.

This is the beginning of a new chapter of your life, "For such a time as this." (Esther 4:14 NIV).

This is your time to become the deliberate creator of your life. This is your time to get the results you want in business and life.

The fact that you have made it to this part of the book tells me something amazing about you!

Thank You!

You are ready to step into your real power and live your true potential.

You are ready to shift how you see yourself, others, and life.

You hold all the power already to create something new and release the burden of control that has held you captive for so long.

Although this journey took me almost half a century to try and figure out, to uncover the truth about how life really works, I want you to have the knowledge and skillsets I wish I had had over thirty-two years ago.

To reveal and quash the misconceptions that are keeping you trapped, feeling as if you go one step forward and two steps back. To make that invisible barrier visible, finally shattering it to release your true power.

I would love to support you in uncovering and living your full potential on the journey of becoming the deliberate creator of your life, to get the results you have always desired.

To begin the journey now, go to:

www.breakthroughtobrilliancebook.com.au.

www.ingramcontent.com/pod-product-compliance
Lightning Source LLC
Chambersburg PA
CBHW072211070526
44585CB00015B/1283